RAMP UP

THE AGENT SCHOOL

A Chad Peevy Company

Domino 2 Technologies, LLC
1801 S. Mopac, Ste 100
Austin, Texas 78746
www.TheAgentSchool.com
(800) 238-1406

Ordering Information:
Quantity sales. Special discounts are available on quantity purchases. For details,
contact the publisher at the address above.

Second Printing, 2018

ISBN 978-1978281752

RAMP UP was created to help real estate agents successfully launch their business. This workbook is a supplement to the online course found at:

TheAgentSchool.com

Access online course at
TheAgentSchool.com

Login name:

Password:

INTRODUCTION

WEEK 1: GET STARTED

WEEK 2: LET'S TALK ABOUT YOU

WEEK 3: MARKETING FOUNDATION

WEEK 4: CREATE CAMPAIGNS

WEEK 5: GO ONLINE

WEEK 6: FARMING

WEEK 7: LISTING PRESENTATION

WEEK 8: TOOLS & LEVERAGE

SET YOUR INTENTION

KELLER-ISMS REFERENCE GUIDE

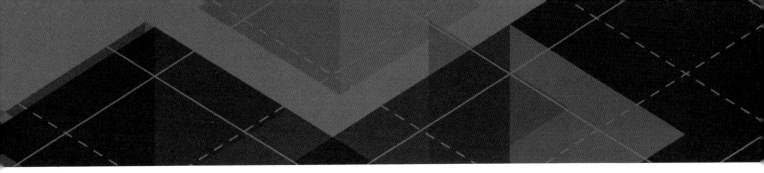

Hello! Welcome to **RAMP UP:** *Rapid Agent Marketing Plan for Ultimate Productivity*.

My name is **Chad Peevy** and I am the founder of **The Agent School** and author of this course.

When you decided to start your real estate business, I imagine that you did so for the income, influence and impact that this industry can afford you. The cold fact of the matter is, an overwhelming number of agents end up quitting. As someone who is in the business of helping real estate agents, it breaks my heart to see agent after agent give up on their dream. **I wanted to help**, so I created this program.

Our common goal through this process is three-fold:

1. Help you navigate all that Keller Williams has to offer you

2. Help you gain rapid momentum to build the business you want

3. Get your first transaction at Keller Williams

Today you can officially say that you have a team of professionals **dedicated to your success**. Together, over the next eight weeks, we are going to get your real estate business launched. Through this program you are getting the benefit of my many years of experience serving thousands of real estate agents, as well as the benefit of your Agent Success Manager *(ASM)* who will be your point of contact throughout this course.

What's going to make the biggest impact is the **community** that you're now a part of — we will connect you with other agents who are working through this course along with you. These agents are going to **help** and **encourage** you throughout this process. I know you'll return the favor.

My new friend – **trust the process**. Don't give up on the program – trust the process. Don't give up on real estate – trust the process. Don't give up on yourself – trust the process. **Trust the process**.

Are you ready to **RAMP UP**?

To your success,

Chad Peevy
Founder and CEO

INTRODUCTION

This is your success list for the introduction of this course. You'll see one of these list at the beginning of each week of RAMP UP. The introduction is going to give you the basis for completing the rest of the course - complete everything on this list before procceding to your Week 1 material.

- ☐ Watch all videos online for this section

- ☐ Set your intention for your business – decide to be present

- ☐ Life Vision Exercise

- ☐ Watch "How This Works" video

- ☐ Decide to be great

- ☐ M.A.P. lesson online

- ☐ Complete your M.A.P.

- ☐ Set up your Google Calendar

- ☐ Time block your week

- ☐ Complete the CGI

LIFE VISION EXERCISE
PERSONAL

SOMEDAY

1.

2.

3.

4.

5.

5-YEAR

1.

2.

3.

4.

5.

1-YEAR

1.

2.

3.

4.

5.

THE AGENT SCHOOL

LIFE VISION EXERCISE
BUSINESS

SOMEDAY

1.

2.

3.

4.

5.

5-YEAR

1.

2.

3.

4.

5.

1-YEAR

1.

2.

3.

4.

5.

YOU ARE WHAT YOU THINK.

YOU ARE WHAT YOU GO FOR.

YOU ARE WHAT YOU DO!

HOW THIS WORKS

Joining Keller Williams is a bit like joining a large university—there are so many opportunities that it can be a challenge to navigate. Universities assign each student an advisor who can help the student navigate the system to get the most tailored, beneficial experience.

As a new associate at Keller Williams, you have many advisors. All the way from the folks at Keller Williams Realty International *(KWRI)* to your local Market Center staff. I hope that you'll consider me and The Agent School as advisors too.

Over the years I have found that many agents new to KW need similar things - this program has been designed to help you navigate those common elements. So for just a little while, eight weeks actually, we're going to help you navigate the world's largest real estate company.

To get you heading in the right direction, I want to give you some instructions for navigating RAMP UP. It's really easy actually—just go page by page. Follow the online lessons one-by-one. That's it. Don't overthink it - just trust that I'm going to get you there.

Every page will tell you what you should be doing. Each chapter of this workbook is one week in the program. The online videos and workbook go hand in hand and will get you successfully through the program.

If you need assistance outside of the weekly office hours, there are a few ways to get some help:

1. Ask your colleagues in the private Facebook Group that has been created for this course *(you'll get instructions for how to join later)*

2. Email us: Hello@TheAgentSchool.com

3. Call us: (800) 238-1406

LIVE LIFE LIKE IT'S RIGGED IN YOUR FAVOR!

WELCOME TO THE GROUP

As you progress throughout this workbook you're going to notice a few icons that will clue you in on what you should be doing:

 Take Action: It's simple - that means there is something to do - something that you can complete and check off your list. Progress feels amazing!

 Watch Video: This icon denotes that there is a corresponding video in your online lessons at TheAgentSchool.com.

During each of the eight weeks of this program you will share online office hours with other KW associates who are going through RAMP UP with you. You'll need to have your weekly success list completed BEFORE your office hours. This way you show up asking the best questions and getting the specific help you need. The weekly office hours are designed to give you the opportunity to share your success and hear how others are finding success.

Your weekly office hours are hosted online. To sign up or access the archives, go to the "Office Hours" tab at TheAgentSchool.com.

I know it's cliché, but it's true….

Together
Everyone
Achieves
More

That's why I give you opportunities to connect with others. Throughout RAMP UP you'll be asked to meet people outside, inside and around your Market Center. One of the most powerful connections you will make will be with your accountability partner. This is the person you're going to work with as you launch your business at Keller Williams.

There's great power in accountability!

THE MONTHLY ACTIVITIES CALENDAR (M.A.P.)

 Watch Video: The M.A.P. *(Monthly Activities Planner)*

 Create your M.A.P.

SET UP YOUR CALENDAR

 Watch Video: Set Up Your Calendar

 Confirm that you can access your Google Calendar via your Keller Williams email address

 Add Google Calendar app to your phone

 Block off personal time for the year *(vacations, holidays, kid events, spouse events)*

 Block off training time for the year *(team meetings, Mega Camp, Family Reunion).*

 Ask your local Market Center staff where you can find a list of local training events for the year.

TIME BLOCKING

 Watch Video: Time blocking

CGI

 Watch Video: Set Up Your CGI

 Complete your CGI - ask your Market Center staff for help.

MAP: MONTHLY ACTIVITIES PLAN

MY ANNUAL GOAL

$ _360,000_ Gross Commission Income *(GCI)*

_48_ transactions at an average of $ _7,500_ per closing

PERSONAL MONTHLY GOALS	BUSINESS MONTHLY GOALS
1.	1. RAMP UP course - weeks 1-4 complete
2.	2. Add _60_ contacts to database
3.	3. ____ representation agreements signed
4.	4. ____ contracts written ____ contracts closed
5.	5.

PERSONAL WEEKLY ACTIVITIES

WEEK 1	WEEK 2	WEEK 3	WEEK 4
1.	1.	1.	1.
2.	2.	2.	2.
3.	3.	3.	3.
4.	4.	4.	4.
5.	5.	5.	5.

BUSINESS WEEKLY ACTIVITIES

WEEK 1	WEEK 2	WEEK 3	WEEK 4
1. RAMP UP Course	1. RAMP UP Course	1. RAMP UP Course	1. RAMP UP Course
2. Accountability partner	2. Open house - shadow	2. Open house - host	2. Create annual plan
3. Complete CGI	3. Inner-sphere announce	3. Outer-sphere announce	3. Update M.A.P. (411)
4. Set up database	4. Touch & feed database	4. Touch & feed database	4. Touch & feed database
5.	5.	5.	5.

WEEK 1:
GET STARTED

This is your success list for the week. To stay on track, complete the tasks listed here before your weekly office hours.

- ☐ Set your intention

- ☐ Find an accountability partner on the RAMP UP Facebook Group

- ☐ Have your first accountability partner meeting

- ☐ 3 professional bios - write or have written

- ☐ Set up a password system

- ☐ Purchase your personal domain

- ☐ Confirm your KW tech is set up properly

- ☐ Get a professional headshot

- ☐ Get your database in order

- ☐ Connect with Chad on social media

- ☐ Meet your Market Center staff

- ☐ Watch all videos online for this section

- ☐ Post your 1 big 'aha' from this week on the Facebook Group Forum

- ☐ Attend RAMP UP office hours – and contribute!

- ☐ Meet with your accountability partner

- ☐ Complete your weekly progress report

PICK AN ACCOUNTABILITY PARTNER

 Watch Video: Accountability Partner

You're going to need an accountability partner. Here's why:

- This is the person you're going to practice your scripts with
- You'll review one another's campaign materials
- Brainstorm partner
- Create an out-of-town referral source
- Make a new friend

 Go to the RAMP UP Facebook Group and post that you need an accountability partner. You may also want to scroll through the feed to see who might have already posted that they need a partner.

Who is your accountability partner? Write their name, email and phone number here:

Crystal Piche

LET'S CONNECT

  Watch Video: Let's Connect

  Follow us on Facebook and Instagram!

Search Facebook for "The Agent School" — there you'll find our LIVE interviews with KW's top producers and thought leaders. For inspirational quotes and the occasional glimpse behind our scenes, our Instagram handle is theagentschool. Don't forget to friend request Chad Peevy and like the Chad Peevy business page so we can stay connected once you finish RAMP UP!

  Join the private Facebook forum for this program! Search Facebook for RAMP UP and request access to the private group.

Please keep in mind that this is a private group and you must answer the entry questions to be granted access.

Once your membership is confirmed you'll want to introduce yourself to the group. Post this info please:

- Your name
- Where you're from
- What you did before real estate
- Why you're excited about being a real estate agent at KW

SEND HANDWRITTEN NOTE CARDS

  Send handwritten notes to 10 people

TALK ABOUT YOUR FUTURE EVERY DAY.

CREATE A PASSWORD VAULT

As a real estate agent you're going to have more than a few logins and passwords. It's good practice to start your business with these login credentials organized somehow. We recommend you take one of these routes:

1) Use a service. There are many – start your search with:

> Dashlane.com, LastPass.com, KeeperSecurity.com, PasswordBoss.com

2) Use a spreadsheet. This is not a secure method and we advise against it - but it works.

 Create password vault

GET YOUR PERSONAL DOMAIN

 Watch Video: Get a Personal Domain

You'll need a personal domain so that it can be forwarded to your KW website. While KW provides agents with a website, some agents will decide to get a custom website – with your own personal domain you won't have to reprint your marketing materials when that change is made. Whether you use the site provided to you or a custom site, we highly recommend that you have a personal domain.

 Go here to get your personal domain: RAMPUPDomain.com

 Save your domain host *(the company from whom you purchased your domain)* and login information in your password vault

PROFESSIONAL BIO

   Watch Video: Professional Bio

You need 3 bios:

Full bio: used in places like your website, perhaps LinkedIn

- Your name, credentials
- Who you serve and how
- Your experience / how you found your way to real estate
- Associations / affiliations
- Community service / how you give back
- Awards / honors / education
- Contact info

Mini-bio: used in places like Facebook, back of postcards, print advertisements

- Your name, credentials
- Who you serve
- 1 interesting thing about you or your company or team

Micro-bio: used in places like Twitter and Instagram

- Name / Company / Web link / Follow me for…. *(use emoji)*

   Write your bio

   Post your mini-bio on the Facebook forum

FULL BIO

- **Your name, credentials**
- **Who you serve and how**
- **Your experience**
- **How you found your way to eeal estate**
- **Associations/Affiliations**
- **Community Service**
- **Awards/Honors/Education**
- **Contact Info**

An accomplished REALTOR® from the heart of Texas, Cindi Nelson has a proven record of successfully representing clients through strategic marketing and a personable approach. Her keen insight and dedication to the best interests of her clients has defined her reputation for being a vital guide through the buying and selling process.

Cindi knew from an early age that she was meant to be a helper. Starting off as president of the student body council, she has spent years advocating for the best interests of her peers. After completing her B.A. at the University of Texas in Austin for Project Administration and Marketing, Cindi was introduced to Keller Williams Realty. In her rookie year as a REALTOR® Cindi closed over $4 million in sales. With a traditional yet effective philosophy, she attributes her success to the three c's: be caring, competent and charming.

In short, Cindi Nelson is a digital savvy people person who knows how to act as a master marketer on her clients' behalf. It is a not just a profession, but a calling to be of service to her community and the Austin area.

MINI-BIO

- **Your name/Credentials/ Company**
- **Who you serve**
- **1 interesting thing about you or your company**

As an accomplished REALTOR® with Keller Williams Realty, Cindi Nelson has a proven record of success. With over $4 million in closed contracts her first year as a real estate agent, Cindi attributes her success to the three c's: be caring, competent and charming. She graduated from the University of Texas with a degree in Project Administration and Marketing. With the experience and education, she is a vital guide in the home buying process as well as a digital savvy people person, prepared to act as a master marketer on her clients' behalf in Austin and surrounding areas.

MICRO-BIO

- **Name/Company/Web link/ Follow me for...**

    (use emoji and keywords)

- Cindi Nelson, REALTOR® at Keller Williams Realty
- CindiNelson.com
- Follow me @CindiRealtor to stay up-to-date on Austin news and events and all things Real Estate.

PROFESSIONAL HEADSHOT

 Watch Video: Professional Headshot

Yes!

- Professionally taken photograph
- Wear solid colors
- Shoot on a white background

No!

- Selfies
- Distracting patterns on clothing
- Do not cut off shoulders or sides of arms in the shot

Be sure that your photographer provides you with the following files and formats:

- PNG – created from full image - with transparent background – this is where you're "cut off" of the background
- JPG – portrait orientation, high resolution
- JPG – square image – used for social media profile image

 Schedule your professional headshot

KW TECH SETUP

  Watch Video: KW Tech Setup

It's really important that your KW technology is set up and functioning properly. This is how you are seen and found by KW associates around the world. There are 100+ steps to a complete tech setup and there are folks that can help you get this done if you don't want to do it yourself.

There are a few ways to get this done:

- DIY – there are a number of videos on KW Connect that will guide you through all of the steps to getting your KW Technology set up. There is a link to these videos in the online portion of RAMP UP.

- Use your Market Center preferred KW Tech Setup service provider – ask your Market Center staff if they have a preferred service provider.

- Order from The Agent Pro Shop – this is our sister company and we can get this step taken care of for you. Visit TheFlyerBoxClub.com or give us a call to get started (800) 238-1406.

Of all the things that need to get done in a KW Tech Setup, the most important one today is your KW email.

  Write your @kw.com email address here:

Since KW has a partnership with Google, your KW email is powered by Gmail. You can send and receive your KW email at gmail.com.

  KW Tech Setup Complete

  Confirm that you can send and receive @kw.com email

YOUR EMAIL SIGNATURE

 Watch Video: Your Email Signature

We prefer that your email signatures be HTML. Large images that span across the bottom of the email, while they may look nice, can create issues for the person receiving the email, especially via mobile phone. Make sure your email signature includes the following:

- Your name, REALTOR®
- Keller Williams Realty
- Your phone (s)
- Your email
- Your personal domain
- Your Market Center address
- (optional) Links to your social media profiles

Some states require that email correspondence include certain disclosures. Ask your Market Center staff if your state has additional requirements.

If you need help with an email signature, we have a complimentary solution you can use to get started available in the online portion of RAMP UP.

Check the online portion of this course for a link to instructions for setting up your email signature in Gmail.

 Set up your email signature

 Watch Video: Your Email Signature

YOUR DATABASE IS YOUR BUSINESS

JUNK IN = JUNK OUT

PULL TOGETHER YOUR DATABASE

   Watch Video: Pull Together Your Database

You'll hear us say often at KW…
Your database is your business.

You'll also hear us say…
What you put in is what you'll get out.
Put junk in and you'll get junk out.

Here are some ways to help you get your contacts gathered:

- MyContactsBackupPro
  This app will take all the contacts on your phone and export them to a spreadsheet. Get the paid version – the free version doesn't have the function to export to .csv and that's what you need.

- Social Media
  Did you know you can export all the contact information for everyone that's connected with you on LinkedIn?

- Your email
  Start pulling the contacts from your email into your database

- Business Cards
  Look in your car, in your desk or sitting on the kitchen counter

- Organization directory
  HOA. Non-profit organization. Your kids school or sports rosters. Did you get a directory?

You're going to pull contacts from these places and others into one single spreadsheet. We have provided you with the template spreadsheet that you need to use. Watch the video for this section for more instructions.

   Download the template spreadsheet and begin entering your contacts

MEET YOUR MARKET CENTER STAFF

Get to know the people supporting you! This week, introduce yourself to every member of your Market Center staff. Here are some questions you might ask them....

- What is your role? What does that mean?
- How did you discover KW?
- What did you do before KW?
- What's the best advice you have for someone in my situation?
- What's your guilty pleasure? *(some day you may want to thank them with a little gift)*
- What's the best book you've read?
- What are the most common traits that you see among successful agents?
- How do you stay motivated?
- What is Family Reunion?
- What is Family Reunion like?
- What is Mega Camp?
- What is Mega Camp like?
- Would you be comfortable sharing your big why?
- Who in the Market Center should I make it a point to meet?

 Watch Video: Meet your Market Center staff

PROGRESS METRICS

DATE: / /								WEEKLY TOTAL:	DATABASE TOTAL CONTACTS:
New contacts added to database:	S	M	T	W	R	F	S		
Appointments:	S	M	T	W	R	F	S		
Contacts added to a conversion campaign:	S	M	T	W	R	F	S		
Agreements signed: (buyer agreement/listing agreement)	S	M	T	W	R	F	S		
Contracts written:	S	M	T	W	R	F	S		
Contracts closed:	S	M	T	W	R	F	S		

NOTES

 Submit your online progress report

THE AGENT SCHOOL

ACCOUNTABILITY PARTNER ACTION

ACTION	I COMPLETED	ACCOUNTABILITY PARTNER COMPLETED
Watch acountability partner online video		
Review success list		

NOTES

WEEK 2:
LET'S TALK ABOUT YOU

This is your success list for the week. To stay on track, complete the tasks listed here before your weekly office hours.

- ☐ Set your intention

- ☐ Create your ideal client profile

- ☐ Define your value proposition

- ☐ Shadow an open house with an experienced agent

- ☐ Practice your "what do you do?" answer

- ☐ Make your inner-sphere announcement

- ☐ Meet two people on your ALC

- ☐ Preview 12 properties

- ☐ Add 10 new people to your database

- ☐ Watch all videos online for this section

- ☐ Post your 1 big 'aha' from this week on the Facebook Group Forum

- ☐ Attend RAMP UP office hours – and contribute!

- ☐ Meet with your accountability partner

- ☐ Complete your weekly progress report

IF YOU BELIEVE IN THE GOAL, YOU'LL PLAY THE ROLE.

DEFINE YOUR VALUE PROPOSITION

 Watch Video: Define Your Value Proposition

Sometimes you get positioned because you didn't take the time to position yourself. When Sally started working in Jane's "turf" Sally made it clear to the market that she donates a portion of her commission checks to the local elementary school. She put pictures of herself presenting those checks to the school kids on social media. She didn't go out and trash the competition, she just took up so much space in the mind of the consumer that Jane got pushed out. Sally positioned herself and because Jane had no position, she was pushed out of the consumer consciousness.

Defining your value proposition can be an exciting opportunity for you to identify your place in the market. It can help you to present a honed message to the public that expresses why they should choose you as their real estate professional. Plan for the long haul.

Some ideas to consider:

What position do you own?
How does your community already think of you?
Is it possible to hook your community with a perception that is already there?

What position do you <u>want</u> to own?
Narrow the focus. A jack of all trades is a master of nothing. If you try to be all things to all people, you wind up with nothing.

Who do you need to beat?
Select a position without a firm owner. Think about your position from the perspective of the competitor. What do you have that they don't?

Do you have enough money?
It takes money to capture mind share. Do you have the staying power?

Do you have the patience?
Take the long view. Building a brand takes time.

Are you an authentic messenger of the position?

Here are some examples of value proposition statements from well-known companies:

- Lyft: Rides in minutes.
- Dollar Shave Club: A great shave for a few bucks a month.
- Vimeo: Make life worth watching.
- Tortuga Backpacks: Everything you need without packing a bag.
- Pinterest: A few *(million)* of your favorite things.

I'll admit that real estate value proposition statements can be really hokey. Try to avoid the hokey. The best real estate value proposition statements that I've seen speak to the person more than the real estate.

This exercise can be challenging for some folks. If you find it to be a tough exercise, that's okay! Take advantage of the resources available to you right now through this course. You have these exercises to guide your thinking, you have your fellow associates on the Facebook forum, you have your Agent Success Manager, and you have your local Market Center team to help you.

There are a few things that I want you to remember as you complete this exercise:

1. You can always change your value proposition.

2. It *should* change. The value you offer right now is different than the value you will offer one year from now.

3. If you're having a hard time identifying your value to the market, you can always demonstrate your value through the value of Keller Williams *(ride their coat-tails so to speak)*.

4. Have fun with this!

 Post your value proposition statement in the Facebook forum

BE THE AUTHOR OF YOUR OWN STORY.

WRITE YOUR INTRODUCTION

   Watch Video: Write Your Introduction

You're going to find yourself at a professional or social event and get the question:

"So, what do you do?"

How are you going to answer?

I want you to have a script to answer that question. Now that you have identified your ideal client and your value proposition, this introduction, or "elevator pitch" should come more easily.

Your introduction should tell the person you're talking to what you do, who you work with, and ask if they know anyone that you could help.

Your introduction should not be more than 20 seconds. Write out your bullet points:

- Who you are?
- What do you do?
- Who do you work with?
- How do you help them?
- Ask them if they know anyone like that who you can help.

   Write your introduction.

   Take your phone and record a video of yourself giving your introduction, then post that video in the Facebook forum.

CREATE VALUE BY CREATING ALIGNMENT

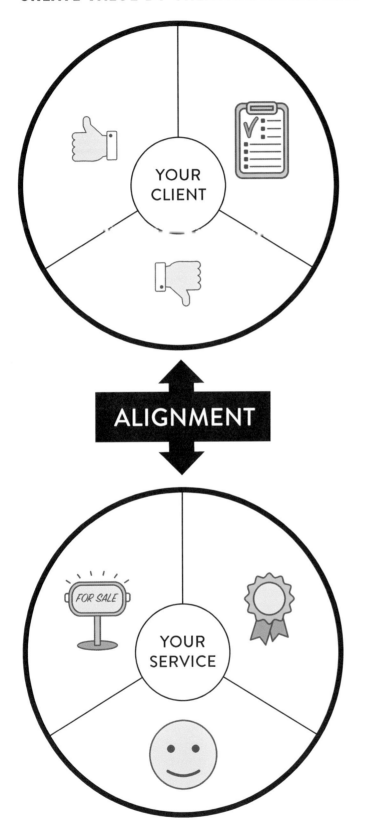

 THE JOB NEEDED

 GAIN

 PAIN

 BENEFITS

 WHAT YOU OFFER

 PAIN RELIEVER

YOUR CLIENT

JOB NEEDED? WHAT ARE THEY TRYING TO GET DONE?

WHAT ARE THEIR PAINS & WHAT ANNOYS THEM ABOUT GETTING THE JOB DONE?

WHAT ARE THE OUTCOMES/RESULTS YOUR CLIENT IS LOOKING FOR?

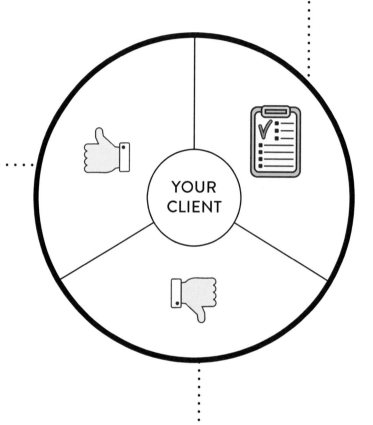

YOUR CLIENT

 THE JOB NEEDED

 GAIN

 PAIN

YOUR SERVICE AND BENEFITS

WHAT DO YOU OFFER?

HOW DOES YOUR SERVICE ALLEVIATE THEIR PAIN?

HOW DOES YOUR SERVICE CREATE THE OUTCOME YOUR CLIENT IS LOOKING FOR?

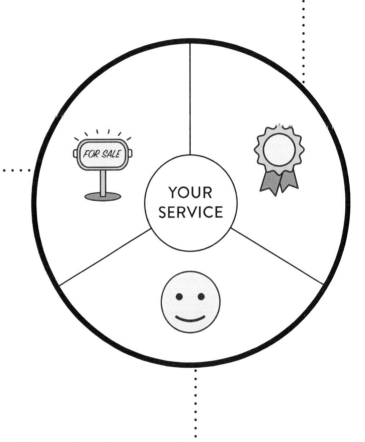

YOUR SERVICE

 THE JOB NEEDED

 GAIN

 PAIN

🖳 IDEAL CLIENT PROFILE

GOALS AND VALUES

Goals:

Values:

CHALLENGES AND PAIN

Challenges:

Pain:

WHERE ARE THEY?

Location:

Gender:

Age:

Language:

What do they read:

What are they interested in:

Where do they work:

Residential status:

Other profile considerations:

PLACE THEIR PHOTO HERE

BEING KIND AND CARING FOR OTHER PEOPLE WILL NEVER GO OUT OF STYLE.

ANNOUCEMENT TO YOUR INNER-SPHERE

Watch Video: Announcement to Your Inner-Sphere

I want you to call your inner-sphere and announce that you are ready to help them with their real estate needs. You should call your 12 closest friends—they don't have to be local. All we're doing is getting you accustomed to talking to people as a real estate professional.

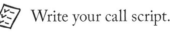 Call your 12 closest friends. Write their names here:

1. _____
2. _____
3. _____
4. _____
5. _____
6. _____
7. _____
8. _____
9. _____
10. _____
11. _____
12. _____

 Write your call script.

Remember to incorporate the introduction you wrote earlier as well as your value proposition, which includes: "Do you know anyone like that who I could help?"

What happened? Easier than you thought? Harder? Did you get a lead?

Post about your experience on the Facebook forum so everyone can learn from your experience.

THE ALC IS A FREE MASTERMIND GROUP.

WHY ARE YOU NOT ATTENTING?

GARY GENTRY
THE FIRST KW AGENT

MEET 2 ON ALC

 Watch Video: Meet Your ALC

What is the ALC? Agent Leadership Council.

The **ALC** acts as the Market Center's Board of Directors. They are the guardians of the culture. These are agents in the Market Center who bring wisdom and perspective to this volunteer leadership role. In most Market Centers, an agent has to be in the top percentage of production in order to be selected to serve on the ALC.

Questions you may ask them:

- What's the best thing I could be doing right now?
- Where do you see the most opportunity for a new agent in our market?
- Who is your go-to resource for local economic information?
- What are the daily habits that have made you successful?
- Do you have a preferred vendor list that you would be willing to share?
- Do you teach any classes here in the Market Center? When is your next class?

 Meet 2 members of your ALC

SEND HANDWRITTEN NOTE CARDS

 Send handwritten notes to 10 people

YOUR DATABASE IS HUNGRY.

FEED IT.

ADD 10 TO YOUR DATABASE

 Watch Video: Feed Your Database

This week and each week thereafter, you need to add 10 new people to your database. This is what we call "feeding your database" – it's hungry!

Here are some ideas to help you feed your database:

- Meetup.com
- EventBrite.com
- Local newspaper to find events in your city
- BNI *(Google it)*
- Rotary Club
- Chamber of Commerce *(large cities will have more than one – Hispanic, LGBT, Asian American, African American, Women's, Young People, and more)*
- Go to a party!

OR

- Connect with people online
- Social networks
- Run an ad like a lead magnet *(know what you're doing!)*
- Start a conversation with friends of friends on Facebook

 Add 10 to database

PREVIEW 12 HOMES

  Watch Video: Property Preview

  Preview 12 homes
Download forms in the online portion of RAMP UP

SHADOW AN OPEN HOUSE

  Watch Video: Shadow an Open House

Find an experienced agent in your Market Center who is hosting an open house this weekend and ask if you can shadow them. Members of your ALC are a good place to start. Remember that you are shadowing them so that you can learn - you are not there to lead generate. Be respectful of their efforts and experience and allow them to do their job.

Take a backseat and just observe. Take note of everything they do. Pay attention to the scripts they use as people come and go. Ask them questions while no one is there looking at the property. How do they collect prospect information? How have they staged the house? What was their strategy for putting out signs? Help them set up and lock up. Be sure to thank them for the experience - you may even want to buy them a coffee.

  Shadow an open house with an experienced agent

PROPERTY PROFILE

Address: 2 Jorgenson Lane, Hampstead NH 03841

Listing Agent: Ian Handel   List Price: 427,000

Bed: 3   Bath: 2   Square Feet: 2,457

Stories: 2   Year Build: 1987   Style:

Smells: Sounds: Lighting:

Features of Note:

Address: 28 Colleen Drive, Salem NH 03079

Listing Agent: Mary-Jo Driggers   List Price: 499,060

Bed: 3   Bath: 13/4   Square Feet: 2,446

Stories: 2   Year Build: 1987   Style: Colonial

Smells: Sounds: Lighting:

Features of Note:

Address: 36 Atkinson Road, Salem NH 03079

Listing Agent: Mark Cooper   List Price: 279,000

Bed: 2   Bath: 2   Square Feet: 1,480

Stories: 3   Year Build: 1988   Style: Condo

Smells: Sounds: Lighting:

Features of Note:

PROGRESS METRICS

DATE: / /	S	M	T	W	R	F	S	WEEKLY TOTAL:	DATABASE TOTAL CONTACTS:
New contacts added to database:									
Appointments:									
Contacts added to a conversion campaign:									
Agreements signed: (buyer agreement/listing agreement)									
Contracts written:									
Contracts closed:									

NOTES

  Submit your online progress report

THE AGENT SCHOOL

ACCOUNTABILITY PARTNER ACTION

ACTION	I COMPLETED	ACCOUNTABILITY PARTNER COMPLETED
Review success list		

NOTES

WEEK 3:
MARKETING FOUNDATION

This is your success list for the week. To stay on track, complete the tasks listed here before your weekly office hours.

- ☐ Set your intention

- ☐ Take a DiSC assessment

- ☐ Validate DiSC with your accountability partner

- ☐ List, Prioritize, Focus worksheet

- ☐ Complete your GPS

- ☐ Announcement to your outer-sphere

- ☐ Host an open house

- ☐ Meet a mortgage broker

- ☐ Preview 12 properties

- ☐ Add 10 new people to your database

- ☐ Watch all videos online for this section

- ☐ Post your 1 big 'aha' from this week on the Facebook Group Forum

- ☐ Attend RAMP UP office hours – and contribute!

- ☐ Meet with your accountability partner

- ☐ Complete your weekly progress report

DISC

 Watch Video: DiSC Personality Profile

The DiSC is a personality assessment. You may have already taken a KPA *(Keller Personality Assessment)* when you interviewed with Keller Williams. The DiSC is a similar tool. We use this tool to help us align your personality with your marketing activities. You'll often hear us talk about marketing from your DiSC. You'll need to complete a DiSC assessment this week. Follow the link in your membership portal to take the assessment. Be sure to allow yourself at least 20 minutes of uninterrupted time to complete the assessment.

The DiSC does not tell us *if* you're going to be a great real estate agent. It only tells us *how* you're going to find your success as a real estate agent.

You'll immediately receive your assessment results via email.

Find the graph referenced to as the "private self" and find the highest two scored letters. Working from left to right, write the first of those two letters here:

I

Write the second letter here:

D

 Complete your DiSC assessment

THE DiSC DOESN'T TELL US IF YOU CAN DO IT –

IT TELLS US HOW YOU WILL GET IT DONE.

DISC VALIDATION

 Watch Video: DiSC Validation

Validating your DiSC can be a powerful exercise in self-discovery. We recommend that you ask your Team Leader or Productivity Coach to validate your DiSC for you. If you're not in a Market Center where that's possible, go through this exercise with your accountability partner.

Find the page in your report titled "Description"—it's the full page narrative. Have the person you've asked to help you validate, read each sentence in the narrative. After the sentence is read, simply indicate whether you agree or disagree with the statement. Put a checkmark next to the sentences that you consider true and cross out the statements with which you disagree.

 Get your DiSC validated

Do you lead with your I or your C?

Are they close to the same? Ask yourself - does talking to people all day charge (I) or drain (C) your batteries?

LIST, PRIORITIZE, FOCUS

 Watch Video: List, Prioritize, Focus

DISC INFORMED MARKETING

THE DRIVE   TEAMWORK

D **S**
I **C**

BE WITH PEOPLE.
LESS DETAIL ORIENTED ACTIVITIES.

(FSBO)	Chamber of Commerce	Just Sold Direct Mail	Pay-per-click
(Expired)	Rotary Club	Just Listed Direct Mail	SEO
(Just Sold)	Meetup.com	Past Clients	(Social Media)
(Just Listed)	Country Club	(Ads)	Search Portals
Past Clients	(Church)	Promotions	Postcard Campaign
Allied Resources	Toastmasters	Allied Resources	Press Releases
(Farm)	Singles Groups	Farm	Advice Columns
(Door-Knocking)	Running Club	Apartments	(Open House)
Client Parties	Rowing Club	Corporations	"Orphaned" Buyers
(Networking Groups)	Alumni Association	Builders	"Orphaned" Sellers
(Social / Community Functions)		Banks	Recruiting for Profit Share
Event Booths		Third-Party Companies	
(Open House)		Investors	
Your Charity		Seminars	
Garage Sales		Teaching / Speaking	
KW RED DAY		Promotions	
Movie Nights		Email	
(Happy Hours)		Review Websites	
Housewarming Parties		Investor Forums	
Volunteer		Create Facebook Groups	
HOA			
PTA			

EVENTS WHERE YOU CAN BE IN
CHARGE. DETAILS.

$$300,000 \times .05 = 15000/2$$

$$7,500$$

48 Transactions

4/Month

LIST, PRIORITIZE, FOCUS

LIST

[Wha]t are you considering, and how much time/money will it take?

PRIORITIZE

6. Just Sold
7. Farm
8. Door Knocking
9. Social Media
10. Ads

3. Open Houses
4. Social/Community functions
5. Just Listed

FOCUS

1.

2.

3.

4.

5.

🖥 MY GPS

MY BIG GOAL

3 PRIORITIES

1.	2.	3.

5 STRATEGIES

1-1	2-1	3-1
1-2	2-2	3-2
1-3	2-3	3-3
1-4	2-4	3-4
1-5	2-5	3-5

FIRST... SET YOUR INTENT

ANNOUNCEMENT TO YOUR OUTER-SPHERE

 Watch Video: Annoucement to Your Outer-Sphere

Your outer-sphere is the 60-70 people that are in your database who you are friendly with but didn't make the cut for your inner-sphere list.

Go back to your List, Prioritize, Focus worksheet. From the activities there, which medium is best suited to deliver your announcement to your outer-sphere? Email? Social media? Phone? Text?

Write that medium here:

If you aren't sure how to use that medium to deliver your message, then research that method online, ask the Facebook forum for help or attend office hours.

Is your message to your outer-sphere the same as your inner-sphere? Do you need to make any adjustments? What did you learn from your announcement to your inner-sphere? Any constructive feedback from those closest friends? Any feedback from the Facebook forum?

 Make adjustments to your announcement script

 Deliver your announcement to outer-sphere

The magic button in real estate is follow-up. If anyone replies to your announcement, especially if you chose email, call them. Tell them how excited you are and give them your introduction script which ends with…. "Do you know anyone like that who I could help?"

EXPECT SOMETHING FROM YOURSELF.

HOST AN OPEN HOUSE

 Watch Video: Host an Open House

Now that you've shadowed an open house, it's time to host your own!

If you don't have your own listing to hold open, that's okay. Contact an agent in your Market Center who has a listing on the market. Ask them if you can hold their listing open.

If you're not quite comfortable after shadowing someone, talk to your Market Center's Productivity Coach, your Team Leader or a member of your ALC. They are all there to help you.

Some agents are going to be very particular about how you conduct an open house for their listing. Be sure you ask them a lot of questions about what they expect. Here are some questions you might consider:

- Is the property occupied?
- Would you like me to coordinate with your seller or would you prefer to do that?
- Is *(day)* from *(time)* okay with you?
- Would you prefer that I use your open house signs or are mine okay? *(we prefer that you use your own if possible)*
- What should I know about this listing?
- Are there any special circumstances or issues with this property that I should know about?
- Is this property in an HOA or city that limits the use of open house signs?
- THANK YOU

OPEN HOUSE CHECKLIST

THREE DAYS BEFORE

Confirm date/time of open house with listing agent.

Print a map of the neighborhood surrounding the open house

Research sign-placement regulations (*HOA, city, county, etc...*)

Run Facebook ads in neighborhood of open house and potential move-up communities nearby

Place Open House Sign in front of house with open day / time

Get 20-30 directional signs and h-wires / stakes

Print 50 flyers (*include map*).

Role-play your scripts with your acccountability partner.

Mark on map where you'll place signs.

TWO DAYS BEFORE

Knock on 100 doors in neighborhood to invite neighbors, leave a flyer at each door.

Advertise the open house on social media

Call anyone in your database who might be interested in this home

Role-play your scripts with your accountability partner.

Compile information on "alternative" properties. Print five copies of each.

> 2-3 properties in a lower price range.
> 2-3 properties in a higher price range.
> 2-3 properties with one more bedroom.
> 1 condominium.

Put together a home book to display. Include in it:

> Property photos
> Details of property
> Tax information
> Survey of lot
> Floor plans
> School information
> Community information (*use resources like Trulia, Zillow and GreatSchools.org to compile your info*)

ONE DAY BEFORE

Assemble your showing kit:

> Bottled water
> Notepads
> Flashlight
> Coloring books and crayons for kids
> Toilet paper
> Tape measure
> Level
> Print, carpet, shingles samples

Review floor plan of house and decide where you'll set up your desk.

Print a guest register and write in two fake names.

Role-play your scripts with your accountability partner.

OPEN HOUSE DAY

Set out your signs - include day / open times on signs
(*do this a few hours before your open house so that you have time to go home and change clothes - setting out signs can be a dirty job*)

Open all the shades - get as much natural light in the home as possible

Turn on all the lights

Check toilets

Look for any potential surprises

Turn on low volume music if appropriate

Set out your flyers / sign in sheet

Get the air circulating - be aware of smells

Clean anything that may need it

SEND HANDWRITTEN NOTE CARDS

    Send handwritten notes to 10 people

MEET A MORTGAGE BROKER

    Watch Video: Meet a Mortgage Broker

Why should you meet with a mortgage broker?

You should have more than one 'go-to' mortgage broker. Let's be intentional this week about meeting one - repeat this step at your first opportunity. Your mortgage broker will be part of your extended team. They are a critical part of the home buying process. A good relationship with your mortgage broker can make or break a deal. They are also one of the first people you will go to when you begin to co-market. For example, you may co-market with your mortgage broker to farm leads or you may co-host events together. Your mortgage broker may also refer leads to you.

Here are some questions you may consider asking:

- How long have you been in the business?
- What were you doing before?
- Who is your ideal client?
- How do you support the Market Center?
- What makes for a good relationship with your best REALTOR®
- How can I help you?
- Who else should I know?

Keep in mind that laws vary in each state—be sure to know the rules when co-marketing with anyone.

PREVIEW 12 HOMES

 Preview 12 homes

ADD 10 TO YOUR DATABASE

This week you need to add 10 new people to your database. This is what we call "feeding your database" – it's hungry!

Here are some ideas to help you feed your database:

- Meetup.com
- EventBrite.com
- Local newspaper to find events in your city
- BNI *(Google it)*
- Rotary Club
- Chamber of Commerce *(large cities will have more than one – Hispanic, LGBT, Asian American, African American, Women's, Young People, and more)*
- Go to a party!

OR

- Connect with people online
- Social networks
- Run an ad like a lead magnet *(know what you're doing!)*
- Start a conversation with friends of friends on Facebook

 Add 10 to database

PROGRESS METRICS

DATE:	/	/								WEEKLY TOTAL:	DATABASE TOTAL CONTACTS:

	S	M	T	W	R	F	S		
New contacts added to database:									

	S	M	T	W	R	F	S		
Appointments:									

	S	M	T	W	R	F	S		
Contacts added to a conversion campaign:									

	S	M	T	W	R	F	S		
Agreements signed: (buyer agreement/listing agreement)									

	S	M	T	W	R	F	S		
Contracts written:									

	S	M	T	W	R	F	S		
Contracts closed:									

NOTES

 Submit your online progress report

THE AGENT SCHOOL

ACCOUNTABILITY PARTNER ACTION

ACTION	I COMPLETED	ACCOUNTABILITY PARTNER COMPLETED
Review success list		

NOTES

WEEK 4:
CREATE CAMPAIGNS

This is your success list for the week. To stay on track, complete the tasks listed here before your weekly office hours.

- ☐ Set your intention

- ☐ Complete your M.A.P. for month 2

- ☐ Create your BUYER Conversion Campaign (8x8)

- ☐ Create your SELLER Conversion Campaign (8x8)

- ☐ Chart your annual plan (33-touch)

- ☐ Meet 2 people in your Market Center

- ☐ Preview 12 properties

- ☐ Add 10 new people to your database

- ☐ Watch all videos online for this section

- ☐ Post your 1 big 'aha' from this week on the Facebook Group Forum

- ☐ Attend RAMP UP office hours – and contribute!

- ☐ Meet with your accountability partner

- ☐ Complete your weekly progress report

THE CONVERSION CAMPAIGN IS...

CALL & RESPONSE

WITH THE PURPOSE TO CONVERT

MARKETING LANGUAGE AT KW

 Watch Video: Marketing Language at KW

THE 7 C'S

 Watch Video: The 7 C's

THE CONVERSION CAMPAIGN

 Watch Video: Conversion Campaigns

 Write your BUYER Conversion Campaign *(8x8)*

 Write your SELLER Conversion Campaign *(8x8)*

THE LONG TERM NURTURE CAMPAIGN

 Watch Video: Long Term Nurture Campaign

 Create your Long Term Nurture Campaign *(33-touch)*

CAMPAIGN FLOW

 Watch Video: Campaign Flow

IDEAL CLIENT LIFE-CYCLE

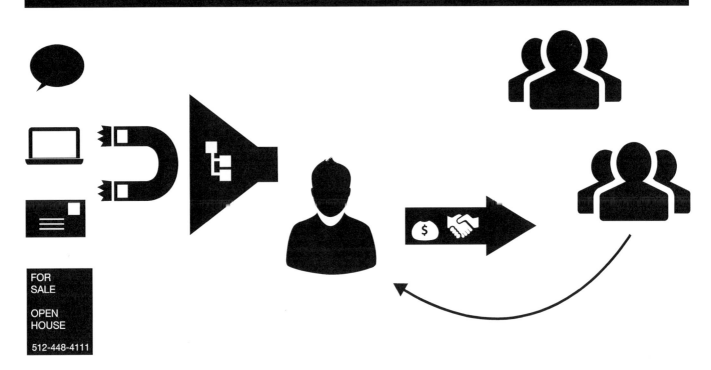

THE 7 C'S

CAST

CAPTURE

CATEGORIZE

CONVERT

CLOSE

CONNECT

COMMUNITY

BUYER CONVERSION CAMPAIGN

MY CONVERSION CAMPAIGN:

Conversion campaigns should follow the _____ & _____ model.

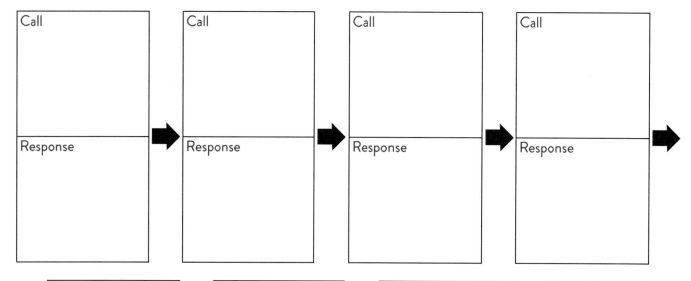

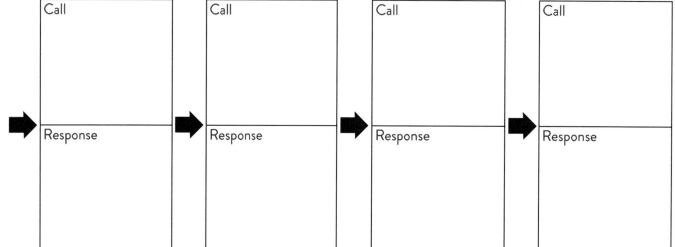

GOAL OF THIS CAMPAIGN:

ONCE YOUR PROSPECT CONVERTS TO YOUR GOAL, THIS CAMPAIGN ENDS. ADD THEM TO YOUR LONG TERM NURTURE

THE AGENT SCHOOL

SELLER CONVERSION CAMPAIGN

MY CONVERSION CAMPAIGN:

Conversion campaigns should follow the _____ & _____ model.

Call	Call	Call	Call
Response	Response	Response	Response

Call	Call	Call	Call
Response	Response	Response	Response

GOAL OF THIS CAMPAIGN:

ONCE YOUR PROSPECT CONVERTS TO YOUR GOAL, THIS CAMPAIGN ENDS. ADD THEM TO YOUR LONG TERM NURTURE

MY ANNUAL PLANNER – TOP OF MIND CAMPAIGN

ANNUAL PLANNER

Should be "evergreen" - content that is specific enough to be valuable, but general enough to be true year after year.

	MONTHLY THEME	WEEK 1	WEEK 2	WEEK 3	WEEK 4
JANUARY					
FEBRUARY					
MARCH					
APRIL					
MAY					
JUNE					
JULY					
AUGUST					
SEPTEMBER					
OCTOBER					
NOVEMBER					
DECEMBER					

THE AGENT SCHOOL

Collect Contact Information

Categorize
(buyer / seller)

Conversion Campaign

Long Term Nurture

TO BE YOUR BEST, YOU HAVE TO LET GO OF THE REST.

PREVIEW 12 HOMES

 Preview 12 homes

ADD 10 TO YOUR DATABASE

This week you need to add 10 new people to your database. This is what we call "feeding your database" – it's hungry!

Here are some ideas to help you feed your database:

- Meetup.com
- EventBrite.com
- Local newspaper to find events in your city
- BNI *(Google it)*
- Rotary Club
- Chamber of Commerce *(large cities will have more than one – Hispanic, LGBT, Asian American, African American, Women's, Young People, and more)*
- Go to a party!

OR

- Connect with people online
- Social networks
- Run an ad like a lead magnet *(know what you're doing!)*
- Start a conversation with friends of friends on Facebook

 Add 10 to database

MEET 2 IN YOUR MARKET CENTER

Meet 2 people in your Market Center that you haven't met yet. It doesn't have to be a formal date, just a meaningful conversation with someone in your Market Center. Here are some things you could ask them....

- How long have you been in the business?
- What's the strangest thing that's ever happened to you as an agent?
- Do you have a specialty? Do you focus on a particular thing?
- What were you doing before real estate?
- Have you ever been to Family Reunion or Mega Camp?
- What made you choose Keller Williams? Did you start your career here?
- What's your big goal for this year?

 Meet 2 people in your Market Center

SEND HANDWRITTEN NOTE CARDS

 Send handwritten notes to 10 people

PROGRESS METRICS

DATE: / /		WEEKLY TOTAL:	DATABASE TOTAL CONTACTS:
	S M T W R F S		
New contacts added to database:			
	S M T W R F S		
Appointments:			
	S M T W R F S		
Contacts added to a conversion campaign:			
	S M T W R F S		
Agreements signed: (buyer agreement/listing agreement)			
	S M T W R F S		
Contracts written:			
	S M T W R F S		
Contracts closed:			

NOTES

 Submit your online progress report

THE AGENT SCHOOL

ACCOUNTABILITY PARTNER ACTION

ACTION	I COMPLETED	ACCOUNTABILITY PARTNER COMPLETED
Review success list		

NOTES

MAP: MONTHLY ACTIVITIES PLAN

MY ANNUAL GOAL

$_____ Gross Commission Income *(GCI)*

_____ transactions at an average of $_____ per closing

PERSONAL MONTHLY GOALS	BUSINESS MONTHLY GOALS
1.	1. RAMP UP course - weeks 5-8 complete
2.	2. Add _____ contacts to database
3.	3. _____ representation agreements signed
4.	4. _____ contract written _____ contracts closed
5.	5.

PERSONAL WEEKLY ACTIVITIES

WEEK 5	WEEK 6	WEEK 7	WEEK 8
1.	1.	1.	1.
2.	2.	2.	2.
3.	3.	3.	3.
4.	4.	4.	4.
5.	5.	5.	5.

BUSINESS WEEKLY ACTIVITIES

WEEK 5	WEEK 6	WEEK 7	WEEK 8
1. RAMP UP Course	1. RAMP UP Course	1. RAMP UP Course	1. RAMP UP Course
2. Touch & feed database	2. Touch & feed database	2. Touch & feed database	2. Update M.A.P. (411)
3.	3.	3.	3. Touch & feed database
4.	4.	4.	4.
5.	5.	5.	5.

THE AGENT SCHOOL

WEEK 5:
GO ONLINE

This is your success list for the week. To stay on track, complete the tasks listed here before your weekly office hours.

- ☐ Set your intention

- ☐ Put the 5-3-2 rule into practice

- ☐ Create your Facebook Business Page

- ☐ Share your KW app with 100 people

- ☐ Preview 12 properties

- ☐ Add 10 new people to your database

- ☐ Watch all videos online for this section

- ☐ Post your 1 big 'aha' from this week on the Facebook Group Forum

- ☐ Attend RAMP UP office hours – and contribute!

- ☐ Meet with your accountability partner

- ☐ Complete your weekly progress report

EVERYONE WHO GOT TO WHERE THEY ARE HAD TO BEGIN WHERE THEY WERE.

ONLINE PRESENCE

 Watch Video: Online presence

CREATE YOUR FACEBOOK BUSINESS PAGE

Why a Facebook Business Page:

- Advertising opportunities
- Analytic reports
- Validity in the social world
- Testimonials / Reviews
- Phone / Email / Website / Market Center Address

Something to remember:

- Follow the same naming rules online as offline. For example, you can't be Chad Peevy REALTY, but you could be Chad Peevy at Keller Williams Realty. Check with your Market Center for naming compliance clarification for your state.

 Update 'where you work' online *(especially LinkedIn, Facebook)*.

The most common places to change "where you work" is Facebook and LinkedIn. By using your Facebook Business Page as 'where you work' rather than just Keller Williams, your friends will be able to easily find a link to your business page from your personal profile.

 Create your Facebook Business Page

SHARE YOUR KW MOBILE APP

The mobile app provided to you by KW is a great piece of technology that your contacts can use on the go. The app is branded to you and is a great tool to keep you top of mind.

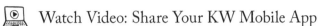 Watch Video: Share Your KW Mobile App

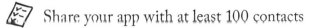 Share your app with at least 100 contacts

SEND HANDWRITTEN NOTE CARDS

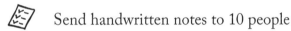 Send handwritten notes to 10 people

PREVIEW 12 HOMES

 Preview 12 homes

5
community

3
business

2
personal

THE 5-3-2 RULE OF POSTING ON FACEBOOK

In the course of a week, follow the 5-3-2 rule....

5 posts: things happening in your community – if possible, how do those things impact the real estate market

3 posts: your business – open houses, new listings, just sold

2 posts: you – you in continuing education classes, you with clients, you with other agents. *(Show your face)*

Engagement opportunities

When you post an article on Facebook think about who would be interested in that post. Tag them in the comments and tell them that you saw this article and thought of them.

 Watch Video: The 5-3-2 Rule of Facebook

 Post your 5-3-2

 Tag someone in your post

 Comment on someone else's post. Engage!

SOCIAL MEDIA TRACKER

FACEBOOK

5 CURATED CONTENT POSTS *(Things happening that your followers care about)*

POST	DAY	TAG SOMEONE	COMMENT
1.			
2.			
3.			
4.			
5.			

3 THINGS ABOUT YOUR BUSINESS *(Open house, new listing, sold, etc.)*

POST	DAY
1.	
2.	
3.	

2 PERSONAL THINGS *(No politics or religion)*

POST	DAY
1.	
2.	

INSTAGRAM *AT LEAST 1 POST AND 1 COMMENT PER DAY*

MONDAY	TUESDAY	WEDNESDAY	THURSDAY	FRIDAY	SATURDAY	SUNDAY
Post	Post	Post	Post	Post	Post	Post
Comment	Comment	Comment	Comment	Comment	Comment	Comment

LINKEDIN *AT LEAST 1X PER WEEKDAY Keep it local.*

MONDAY	TUESDAY	WEDNESDAY	THURSDAY	FRIDAY
1.	1.	1.	1.	1.
Engage Someone	Engage Someone	Engage Someone	Engage Someone	Engage Someone

TWITTER *2X DAILY (OR MORE IF YOU CAN) If you can't create, curate. Keep it local.*

MONDAY	TUESDAY	WEDNESDAY	THURSDAY	FRIDAY	SATURDAY	SUNDAY
1.	1.	1.	1.	1.	1.	1.
2.	2.	2.	2.	2.	2.	2.
Engage Someone	Engage Someone	Engage Someone	Engage Someone	Engage Someone	Engage Someone	Engage Someone

MEET 2 IN YOUR MARKET CENTER

Meet 2 people in your Market Center that you haven't met yet. It doesn't have to be a formal date, just a meaningful conversation with someone in your Market Center. Here are some things you could ask them....

- How long have you been in the business?
- What's the strangest thing that's ever happened to you as an agent?
- Do you have a specialty? Do you focus on a particular thing?
- What were you doing before real estate?
- Have you ever been to Family Reunion or Mega Camp?
- What made you choose Keller Williams? Did you start your career here?
- What's your big goal for this year?

 Meet 2 people in your Market Center

ADD 10 TO YOUR DATABASE

This week you need to add 10 new people to your database. This is what we call "feeding your database" – it's hungry!

Here are some ideas to help you feed your database:

- Host a mastermind with other business owners in your database - ask them to bring another business owner.
- Host a happy hour for your friends - ask them to bring a friend.

 Add 10 to database

PROGRESS METRICS

DATE:	/ /		WEEKLY TOTAL:	DATABASE TOTAL CONTACTS:

	S	M	T	W	R	F	S		
New contacts added to database:									
Appointments:	S	M	T	W	R	F	S		
Contacts added to a conversion campaign:	S	M	T	W	R	F	S		
Agreements signed: (buyer agreement/listing agreement)	S	M	T	W	R	F	S		
Contracts written:	S	M	T	W	R	F	S		
Contracts closed:	S	M	T	W	R	F	S		

NOTES

 Submit your online progress report

ACCOUNTABILITY PARTNER ACTION

ACTION	I COMPLETED	ACCOUNTABILITY PARTNER COMPLETED
Review success list		

NOTES

WEEK 6:
FARMING

This is your success list for the week. To stay on track, complete the tasks listed here before your weekly office hours.

☐   Set your intention

☐   Define your farm(s)

☐   Make a branding decision

☐   Meet a title company representative or closing attorney

☐   Preview 12 properties

☐   Add 10 new people to your database

☐   Watch all videos online for this section

☐   Post your 1 big 'aha' from this week on the Facebook Group Forum

☐   Attend RAMP UP office hours – and contribute!

☐   Meet with your accountability partner

☐   Complete your weekly progress report

DISCIPLINE GIVES YOU FREEDOM

FARMING

 Watch Video: Farming

 Identify your farm

 How will you reach your farm?

 Describe your farm here:

_____

_____

_____

_____

_____

_____

_____

SEND HANDWRITTEN NOTE CARDS

 Send handwritten notes to 10 people

THERE IS NO TRAFFIC AFTER THE EXTRA MILE

 Watch Video: Branding Decision

LEAD WITH YOU

Pros:

- It's awesome to have a personal brand
- Stand out from everyone else
- You control the style / personality of your client experience through the visuals
- It can travel with you should you leave KW
- It builds your own name recognition in a personal business

Cons:

- Your name may not be as well-known as Keller Williams
- A personal brand may costs more than using KW's brand *(to start)*
- You have to maintain your brand standards *(important when you have a team).*

LEAD WITH KW

Pros:

- You get to ride the KW name recognition
- Lead with your affiliation to a large firm and resources it affords
- There are a lot of pre-designed resources available to you

Cons:

- You lose control of your own image
- You may lose the perception of independence and this may matter when competing for a listing where more than one KW agent is interviewing
- KW corporate doesn't market your business. You need to know if your local Market Center spends money to market the KW brand for you

Select one:

☐ **YOU**, backed by the power KW?

OR

☐ **KW**, backed by the power of you?

MEET A TITLE COMPANY REPRESENTATIVE

   Watch Video: Meet a Title Company Rep or Closing Attorney

In most states, your title company representative is like a librarian. They have a wealth of information at their disposal. Get to know your title company representative well—they can be a great resource for you. Want to know how many homes in that neighborhood sold last year and you don't have time to run the numbers yourself? Your title rep can help.

As with a mortgage broker, you'll have more than one title company rep relationship. Go meet at least two more title company reps at your convenience.

No title companies in your state? No worries! Go meet whomever is responsible for closing your transactions.

Here are some questions you may consider asking your title rep:

- How long have you been in the business?
- Do you have any marketing collateral that I could use to supplement my listing package?
- Do you have a buyer's package that I could use?
- Do you have a relocation guide that I could use?
- Are there any economic update events that I should have on my calendar?
- Do you know of any CE *(continuing education)* courses that I should have on my calendar?
- Who else should I know?
- How can I help you?

   Meet a title representative or closing attorney

Beware, just like with mortgage brokers, your relationship with your title rep is regulated. Don't get yourself in trouble. Know the rules.

PREVIEW 12 HOMES

 Preview 12 homes

ADD 10 TO YOUR DATABASE

This week you need to add 10 new people to your database. This is what we call "feeding your database" – it's hungry!

Here are some ideas to help you feed your database:

- Meetup.com
- EventBrite.com
- Local newspaper to find events in your city
- BNI *(Google it)*
- Rotary Club
- Chamber of Commerce *(large cities will have more than one – Hispanic, LGBT, Asian American, African American, Women's, Young People, and more)*
- Go to a party!

OR

- Connect with people online
- Social networks
- Run an ad like a lead magnet *(know what you're doing!)*
- Start a conversation with friends of friends on Facebook

 Add 10 to database

PROGRESS METRICS

DATE:	/	/		WEEKLY TOTAL:	DATABASE TOTAL CONTACTS:

	S	M	T	W	R	F	S		
New contacts added to database:									
Appointments:	S	M	T	W	R	F	S		
Contacts added to a conversion campaign:	S	M	T	W	R	F	S		
Agreements signed: (buyer agreement/listing agreement)	S	M	T	W	R	F	S		
Contracts written:	S	M	T	W	R	F	S		
Contracts closed:	S	M	T	W	R	F	S		

NOTES

 Submit your online progress report

ACCOUNTABILITY PARTNER ACTION

ACTION	I COMPLETED	ACCOUNTABILITY PARTNER COMPLETED
Review success list		

NOTES

WEEK 7:
LISTING PRESENTATION

This is your success list for the week. To stay on track, complete the tasks listed here before your weekly office hours.

☐ Set your intention

☐ Create your listing presentation

☐ Practice your listing presentation with your accountability partner

☐ Update your GPS

☐ Check in with your Team Leader

☐ Preview 12 properties

☐ Add 10 new people to your database

☐ Watch all videos online for this section

☐ Post your 1 big 'aha' from this week on the Facebook Group Forum

☐ Attend RAMP UP office hours – and contribute!

☐ Meet with your accountability partner

☐ Complete your weekly progress report

BEING GREAT STARTS WITH THE DECISION TO BE SO.

MAKE THAT DECISION.

LISTING PRESENTATION

 Watch Video: Listing Presentation

There is no shortage of listing presentation templates out there for you. It really doesn't matter where it comes from, just make sure that you are using material that is true to the way you do business.

Your listing presentation should be visually appealing. When you sit down in front of that seller, or send them your listing presentation ahead of time, you need to be proud of that presentation.

We recommend that you use a listing presentation oriented horizontally so that you can present it on your iPad or other tablet computer. Visit TheAgentSchool.com for our template. It's free for you to personalize and use.

Most agents will have a standard listing presentation that they will put on their tablet or print. This presentation won't change from listing to listing. You may change your approach, but the documents won't. To supplement that listing presentation, agents will print property specific materials that they take on the listing presentation. It's rare to create a custom listing presentation for each listing appointment. That would be a lot of work.

Something to consider:

- Create in Google Slides so that it's backed up and you can access from any Internet connected device

 Create your listing presentation

LISTING PRESENTATION SCRIPT PRACTICE

By now you should have your listing presentation ready. Please keep in mind, the first time you do this will be different than every other time you do it. It's okay *(and expected)* that you're going to make changes to your listing presentation. So don't fret about getting it perfect—no amount of work will get it perfect. You don't yet know what you don't know!

Practicing with your accountability partner will get rid of some of those jitters—not all, but some. It's also going to highlight which areas could use some tweaking or beefing up. Have fun with your listing presentation practice.

Here are some tips for your practice session.

1. Feedback is a gift. When your accountability partner gives you feedback, don't discount their gift by making excuses. Just say "thank you." You get to decide whether their feedback is worth incorporating.

2. Nothing is "wrong." There will likely be plenty of opportunities to point out how something might be done differently, but nothing is "wrong."

3. Don't go negative. Encourage one another and every opportunity for improvement. Try to point out two things that your partner did well.

I encourage you to present for one another via video, not phone. Set up your computer so that you can see from waist up just as if you were sitting with a seller at their kitchen table. Dress appropriately and make this as real as possible. Here are some tools that you can use for video calls:

- Facetime
- Google Hangouts
- Join.me
- Zoom.us

PREVIEW 12 HOMES

 Preview 12 homes

ADD 10 TO YOUR DATABASE

This week you need to add 10 new people to your database. This is what we call "feeding your database" – it's hungry!

Here are some ideas to help you feed your database:

- Meetup.com
- EventBrite.com
- Local newspaper to find events in your city
- BNI *(Google it)*
- Rotary Club
- Chamber of Commerce *(large cities will have more than one – Hispanic, LGBT, Asian American, African American, Women's, Young People, and more)*
- Go to a party!

OR

- Connect with people online
- Social networks
- Run an ad like a lead magnet *(know what you're doing!)*
- Start a conversation with friends of friends on Facebook

 Add 10 to database

CHECK IN WITH YOUR TEAM LEADER

 Watch Video: Check in with your Team Leader

It's important to have a good relationship with your Team Leader. They are one of your biggest champions in your business. Make it a habit to check in with your team leader to ask for opportunities to serve your Market Center. The more you give this relationship, the more you'll get out of it.

Here are some things you may want to ask your Team Leader:

- Who else should I know?
- Any training opportunities coming up that I should know about?
- How can I help you?
- Any committees looking for extra help?
- Do you know anyone looking to buy or sell?
- What am I missing?

 Check in with your Team Leader

SEND HANDWRITTEN NOTE CARDS

 Send handwritten notes to 10 people

MY GPS

MY BIG GOAL

3 PRIORITIES		
1.	2.	3.

5 STRATEGIES		
1-1	2-1	3-1
1-2	2-2	3-2
1-3	2-3	3-3
1-4	2-4	3-4
1-5	2-5	3-5

PROGRESS METRICS

DATE:	/	/							WEEKLY TOTAL:	DATABASE TOTAL CONTACTS:

	S	M	T	W	R	F	S		
New contacts added to database:									
Appointments:	S	M	T	W	R	F	S		
Contacts added to a conversion campaign:	S	M	T	W	R	F	S		
Agreements signed: (buyer agreement/listing agreement)	S	M	T	W	R	F	S		
Contracts written:	S	M	T	W	R	F	S		
Contracts closed:	S	M	T	W	R	F	S		

NOTES

 Submit your online progress report

ACCOUNTABILITY PARTNER ACTION

ACTION	I COMPLETED	ACCOUNTABILITY PARTNER COMPLETED
Review success list		

NOTES

WEEK 8:
TOOLS & LEVERAGE

This is your success list for the week. To stay on track, complete the tasks listed here before your weekly office hours.

☐ Set your intention

☐ Complete your M.A.P. for month 3

☐ Ask 25 people for referrals

☐ Post your 3 big 'aha' moments from RAMP UP on the Facebook Group Forum

☐ Preview 12 properties

☐ Add 10 new people to your database

☐ Watch all videos online for this section

☐ Post your 1 big aha from this week on the Facebook Group Forum

☐ Meet with your accountability partner

☐ Complete your weekly progress report

ASK MORE QUESTIONS

ADD 10 TO YOUR DATABASE

This week you need to add 20 new people to your database. This is what we call "feeding your database" – it's hungry!

Here are some ideas to help you feed your database:

- Meetup.com
- EventBrite.com
- Local newspaper to find events in your city
- BNI *(Google it)*
- Rotary Club
- Chamber of Commerce *(large cities will have more than one – Hispanic, LGBT, Asian American, African American, Women's, Young People, and more)*
- Go to a party!

OR

- Connect with people online
- Social networks
- Run an ad like a lead magnet *(know what you're doing!)*
- Start a conversation with friends of friends on Facebook

 Add 10 to database

GET PLUGGED IN

 Watch Video: Get Plugged-in at KW

MEET 2 IN YOUR MARKET CENTER

Meet 2 people in your Market Center that you haven't met yet. It doesn't have to be a formal date, just a meaningful conversation with someone in your Market Center. Here are some things you could ask them....

- How long have you been in the business?
- What's the strangest thing that's ever happened to you as an agent?
- Do you have a specialty? Do you focus on a particular niche?
- What were you doing before real estate?
- Have you ever been to Family Reunion or Mega Camp?
- What made you choose Keller Williams? Did you start your career here?
- What's your big goal for this year?

 Meet 2 people in your Market Center

SEND HANDWRITTEN NOTE CARDS

 Send handwritten notes to 10 people

DATABASE MANAGEMENT

 Watch Video: Database Management

DATABASE MANAGEMENT TOOL EVALUATION

OFFLINE	**MASS EMAIL**	**BASIC CRM**	**ADVANCED CRM**	**ENTERPRISE CRM**
Index cards	Mailchimp	eEdge / Market Leader	Brivity	SalesForce
	Constant Contact	Insightly	Realvolve	Netsuite
	Emma	The Wise Agent	LionDesk	
			Infusionsoft	
			TopProducer	

CRM =
Customer Relationship Management

SOLUTION	SETUP	MONTHLY	TIME	SKILL	TEAM	AUTO

GET PLUGGED-IN AT KW

GET CONNECTED *(Like going to a big university)*

- Market Center Classes

- KW Connect

- Team Meeting

- Mastery Series Events

- Market Center Committees

- Create your own accountability groups

- Market Center Events
  - see Intranet calendar

- Look for ways to be of service

- KW Cares

- RED Day

ADDITIONAL FEES *(May be required)*

- MAPS Coaching

- BOLD

- KWRI Events - Test Courses

- Market Center Productivity Coaching

- MegaCamp

- Family Reunion

- The Agent School

REQUIRES MEMBERSHIP OR QUALIFICATIONS

THE AGENT SCHOOL

MAP: MONTHLY ACTIVITIES PLAN

MY ANNUAL GOAL

PERSONAL MONTHLY GOALS	BUSINESS MONTHLY GOALS
1.	1.
2.	2.
3.	3.
4.	4.
5.	5.

PERSONAL WEEKLY ACTIVITIES

WEEK 1	WEEK 2	WEEK 3	WEEK 4
1.	1.	1.	1.
2.	2.	2.	2.
3.	3.	3.	3.
4.	4.	4.	4.
5.	5.	5.	5.

BUSINESS WEEKLY ACTIVITIES

WEEK 1	WEEK 2	WEEK 3	WEEK 4
1.	1.	1.	1.
2.	2.	2.	2.
3.	3.	3.	3.
4.	4.	4.	4.
5.	5.	5.	5.

THE AGENT SCHOOL

PROGRESS METRICS

DATE:	/	/							WEEKLY TOTAL:	DATABASE TOTAL CONTACTS:

	S	M	T	W	R	F	S		
New contacts added to database:									

	S	M	T	W	R	F	S	
Appointments:								

	S	M	T	W	R	F	S	
Contacts added to a conversion campaign:								

	S	M	T	W	R	F	S	
Agreements signed: (buyer agreement/listing agreement)								

	S	M	T	W	R	F	S	
Contracts written:								

	S	M	T	W	R	F	S	
Contracts closed:								

NOTES

 Submit your online progress report

ACCOUNTABILITY PARTNER ACTION

ACTION	I COMPLETED	ACCOUNTABILITY PARTNER COMPLETED
Review success list		
How do we maintain our momentum?		

NOTES

INWARD FIRST,
THEN ONWARD
AND UPWARD!

SET YOUR INTENTION

DATE	DAILY INTENTION

SET YOUR INTENTION

DATE	DAILY INTENTION

THE AGENT SCHOOL

SET YOUR INTENTION

DATE	DAILY INTENTION

SET YOUR INTENTION

DATE	DAILY INTENTION

SET YOUR INTENTION

DATE	DAILY INTENTION

SET YOUR INTENTION

DATE	DAILY INTENTION

YOU HAVE MY PERMISSION TO RESET YOUR AMBITION.

KELLER-ISMS REFERENCE GUIDE

12-Direct: *(twelve direct)* Marketing campaign for people you have not yet met - a farm. Twelve touches over the course of twelve months. The purpose of a 12-direct is to entice a prospective buyer or seller to engage the agent – to take them from a 'have not met' to a 'met.' The agent would then place the contact on a conversion campaign campaign.

33-touch: *(thirty three touch)* In RAMP UP, we refer to this as your long term nurture campaign. A campaign whose purpose is to keep you top-of-mind with your database. Everyone in your database should be on a 33-touch campaign. These are people whom you have met.

4-1-1: *(four one one)* In RAMP UP, we refer to this as a M.A.P. A productivity tool – think of "goal setting to the now." Numbers represent 4 weeks, 1 month, 1 year as the 4-1-1 form breaks 1 annual goal down to 1 month goals, and then 4 weeks of activities that you would engage in order to realize those goals.

8x8: *(eight by eight)* In RAMP UP, we refer to this as a conversion campaign. Traditionally considered 8 touches in 8 weeks. A call and response campaign whose purpose is to convert a person you recently met to a client. The 8x8 campaign conversion is a signed buyer agreement or signed listing agreement. Should the person you've placed on an 8x8 campaign sign an agreement before the 8 touches have been executed, they simply fall off that campaign and are placed on a 33-touch campaign.

ALC: Agent Leadership Council – Can be thought of as the Market Center's board of directors. Made up of top producers in the Market Center who have volunteered to serve in this role.

Capper: An agent who has paid in their maximum contribution to the company for their fiscal year. You may hear agents say they've 'capped' – this means that they will receive a greater percentage of their commissions for the remainder of their fiscal year.

eEDGE: *(eee-edge)* – A collection of online tools made available to you from Keller Williams – may be accessed through your KW Dashboard *(mykw.kw.com)*

Farm: A chosen group of potential home buyers and sellers. These are people an agent hasn't yet met, but meet at least one condition of an agent's ideal client profile.

GCI: Gross Commission Income – The total amount of commission dollars received from a transaction.

KWLS: Keller Williams Listing Service

KWU: Keller Williams University

MAPS: Mega Agent Productivity Systems. Keller Williams coaching company.

MC: Market Center – A Keller Williams real estate office. Typically full of eager minds and awesome talent.

MCA: Market Center Administrator – Market Center staff person who is responsible for implementing and maintaining all operating systems in the Market Center. Many MCA's function as the CFO of a Market Center.

MREA: Millionaire Real Estate Agent – Book written by Gary Keller, also referred to as "The Red Book." It is a must read for anyone in real estate.

OP: Operating Principal – Market Center ownership. Responsible for the success of the Market Center.

PC: Productivity Coach – Market Center staff responsible for helping agents realize their full potential in real estate. PC roles and functions vary from Market Center to Market Center.

TL: Team Leader – Can be thought of as the CEO of the Market Center. The Team Leader is typically responsible for recruiting new agents to the Market Center.

WI4C2TS: *(why four see two tees)* – The Keller Williams belief system.

CUSTOMIZE YOUR LIFE EXPERIENCE

CLARITY DOESN'T JUST COME IT IS SOUGHT

I AM FEARLESS BECAUSE I HAVE CONFIDENCE IN MY ABILITY TO FIGURE THINGS OUT

TALK ABOUT YOUR FUTURE EVERY DAY

BEING GREAT IS A DECISION
MAKE THAT DECISION

CONTRIBUTE – AND DO IT DAMN WELL

NOT EVERY MOUNTAIN IS WORTH THE CLIMB

TO BE YOUR BEST YOU HAVE TO LET GO OF THE REST

WHEN YOU KNOW THE GOAL – YOU'LL PLAY THE ROLE

FIND THE FUN

YOU HAVE MY PERMISSION TO RESET YOUR AMBITION

SATISFACTION COMES FROM CONTRIBUTION

LIVE LIFE LIKE IT'S RIGGED IN YOUR FAVOR

DECIDE

EXPECT SOMETHING FROM YOURSELF

I WRITE MY OWN STORY

CARING ABOUT OTHER PEOPLE WILL NEVER GO OUT OF FASHION

WHY ARE YOU OK BEING "OK"?

"APPROPRIATE" ISN'T A WORD YOU WANT ON YOUR TOMBSTONE

UPWARD ONWARD INWARD

WIN THE MORNING

DISCIPLINE GIVES YOU FREEDOM

SELF-EXPRESSION IS THE GATEWAY TO HAPPINESS

PRODUCTIVITY DETACHED FROM YOUR PURPOSE IS JUST BUSY WORK

YOU CAN'T REACH A HIGHER LEVEL WITHOUT A HIGHER LEVEL OF AMBITION

FIRST SET YOUR INTENT

LEVEL

WE OPERATE AT A WORLD-CLASS

THE TRUTH WILL SET YOU FREE BUT FIRST IT WILL PISS YOU OFF

95989649R10066

Made in the USA
Columbia, SC
20 May 2018